Little Sister

D1066550

Photo Scrapbook

ANN M. MARTIN

SCHOLASTIC INC.
New York Toronto London Auckland Sydney

The author gratefully acknowledges
Nancy E. Krulik
for her help
with this book.

Cover art by Susan Tang
Interior art by John DeVore

ISBN 0-590-92194-0

12 11 10 9 8 7 6 5 4 3 2 1   6 7 8 9/9 0

Printed in the U.S.A.
First Scholastic printing, July 1996

HOORAY FOR ME!

name is _____.

m _____ years old.

ke this picture of me because _____
_____.

FAMILY FUN!

Some kids have one family. But not Karen and her brother Andrew. They have two families, a big-house family and a little-house family.

This is a picture of my family.

These are the names of the people in my family: _____

_____

HOME SWEET HOME

ren's big and little houses are both in the town of Stoneybrook, Connecticut. Karen and drew spend one month at the big house and the next month at the little house.

This is a picture of my home.

y address is:_____

FRIENDS AND NEIGHBORS

Stoneybrook is filled with nice people. There is Mrs. Ramirez, the letter carrier; Mr. Wils
the bus driver; and Mrs. Porter, Karen's big-house neighbor.

Here are pictures of two special people in my neighborhood.

This is a picture of _____

is is a picture of _____.

ANIMAL PALS

Karen has lots of stuffed animals. She also has some real live pets—a rat named En[...] Junior and a goldfish named Crystal Light the Second.

This is a picture of my pet.

I have _____ pet(s) named _____

_____

FRIENDS FOREVER!

*ren has two best friends, Hannie Papadakis and Nancy Dawes. Karen, Hannie, and
ncy call themselves the Three Musketeers. All for one and one for all!*

This is a picture of my best friend.

best friend's name is_____.

ese are some of the things my best friend and I like to do together: _____

_____

LET'S BIKE!

Karen has a brand-new bicycle, a pink and purple two-wheeler.

This is a picture of me on my bicycle.

My favorite place to ride my bike is _____

GOOD SPORTS

"...ome Run" Karen is the star player on her softball team, Kristy's Krushers. The Krushers ...ay against their rivals, Bart's Bashers.

This is a picture of me playing my favorite sport.

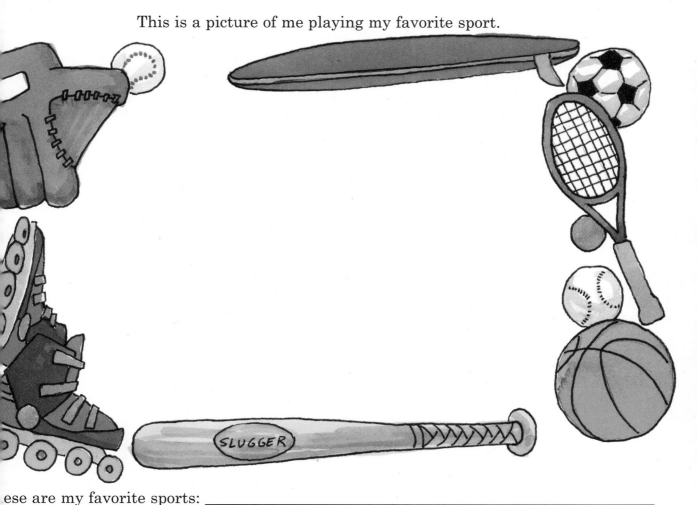

...ese are my favorite sports: _____

...e sport I'm best at is _____.

TRAVELING ALONG

Summer is a special time for Karen. One summer the Three Musketeers stayed in a cal near Shadow Lake. Another time Karen visited her grandparents' farm.

This is a picture from my trip.

Having a great time. Wish you were here!

POST CARD

This summer my family took a trip to _____

The part of the trip I liked best was _____

_____

CAMP IS COOL!

cky Karen. She spent a whole week at Camp Mohawk! While she was there, Karen went rseback riding, swimming, and camping. She also learned some scary campfire stories.

This is a picture taken at camp.

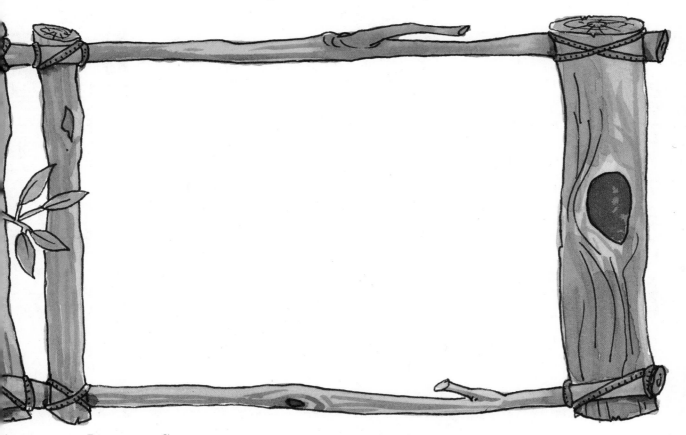

is summer I went to Camp _____.

ese are the names of the friends I made:_____

_____

SCHOOL TIME

Karen goes to Stoneybrook Academy. She is in the second grade.

This is a picture of my school, _____.

I am in the _____ grade.

There are _____ kids in my class.

HEY, TEACH!

...ren loves her teacher, Ms. Colman. Ms. Colman never yells, and she makes learning fun.

...is is a picture of my teacher, _____.

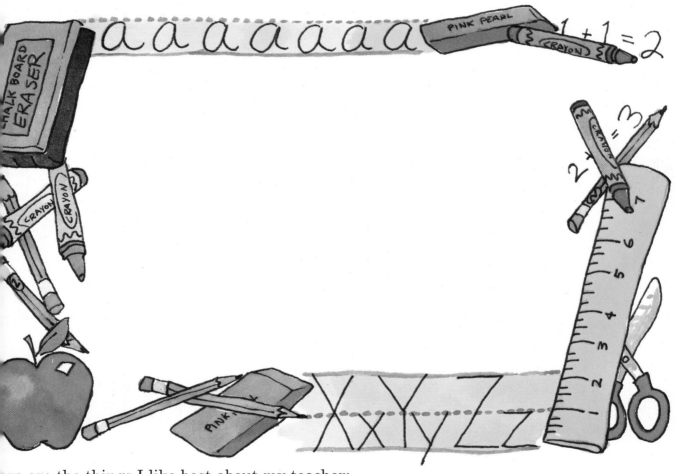

...ere are the things I like best about my teacher: _____

_____

RECESS IS BEST!

Karen loves the playground at school. The Three Musketeers play hopscotch, jacks, or free tag during recess.

This is a picture taken during recess.

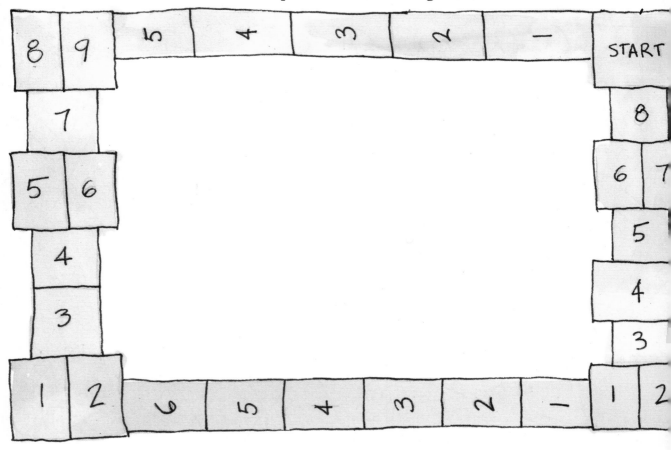

I like to spend recess with _____

My favorite playground game is _____

FUNNY PHOTOS

ren loves to act silly. Sometimes she plays jokes on her classmates. Other times she dresses in funny clothes. One time she directed a silly movie called Princess Gigglepuss.

Here is a picture of my friends and me acting silly!

HOORAY FOR CLASS TRIPS!

Ms. Colman took Karen's class to the zoo. Where did your teacher take you?

Here is a picture from my class trip.

My class went on a trip to _____

On the bus, I sat next to _____

I was so excited to see _____

ALL YEAR ROUND

ren loves every season. In the summer, she swims. In the autumn, she carves pumpkins. the winter, she ice-skates. And when spring comes, Karen plants flowers.

Each of these next four pictures was taken during a different season.

SUMMER

is is a picture of _____.

was taken on _____.

This is a picture of _____

It was taken on _____

is is a picture of _____.

was taken on _____.

This is a picture of _____

It was taken on _____

HAPPY BIRTHDAY, U.S.A.!
(and Canada, too)

ren loves holidays. Luckily for her, there are holidays all year long! In the summer, thing beats the Stoneybrook Fourth of July celebration.

This is a picture of me on the Fourth of July (or Canada Day, July first.)

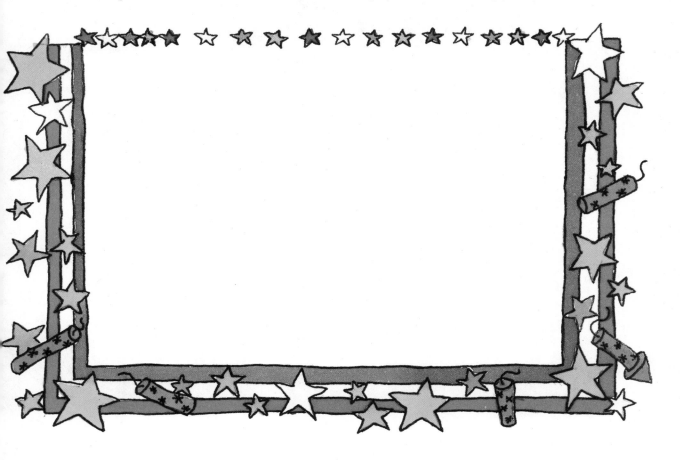

pent the day _____.

TRICK OR TREAT!

Karen loves dressing up as a witch for Halloween. She also likes being a monster and a gh[

This is a picture of me on Halloween. I dressed up as _____

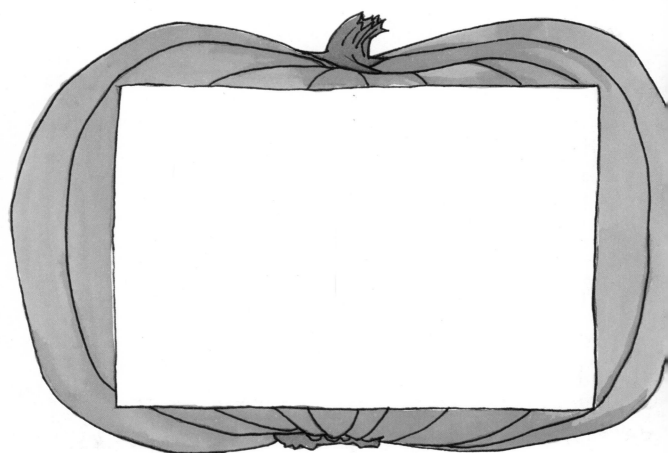

This year I went trick-or-treating with _____

The best treat I got was _____

GIVING THANKS

ren is always thankful for Thanksgiving. She loves turkey. One year, though, she had two anksgiving dinners—in one day. All that turkey gave her a gigundo stomachache!

This is a picture taken on Thanksgiving day.

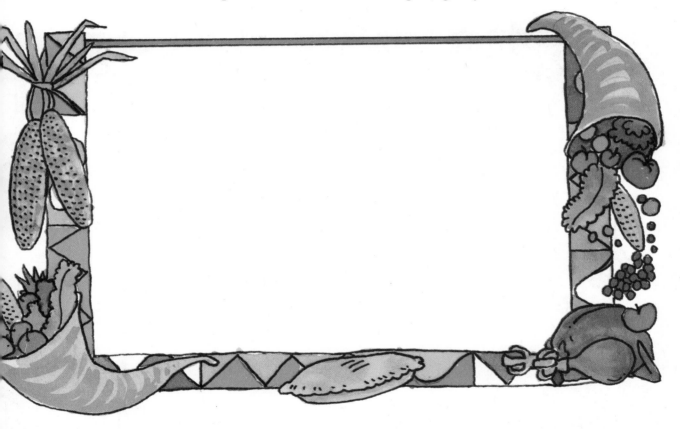

elebrated Thanksgiving at _____.

ese are some of the things I ate: _____

re are a few of the things I am thankful for: _____

HO-HO-HO HOLIDAYS!

Karen loves celebrating Christmas with her family. Holiday time is extra special becau
Karen gets to celebrate Hanukkah with Nancy Dawes, and Kwanzaa with Sara Ford.

This is a picture of my family celebrating a winter holiday.

The best part about the holiday season is _____

BE MY VALENTINE

2 good 2 B 4-gotten. *That's what Ricky Torres wrote in his Valentine's Day card to Karen.*

This is a picture of my valentine.

valentine's name is _____.

ke my valentine because _____.

HAPPY BIRTHDAY TO ME!

*When Karen turned seven, she had two birthday parties: a fancy, dress-up dinner at the l...
house and a circus party with her big-house family.*

Here is a picture of me on my birthday.

My birthday is on _____

I am now _____ years old.

This is where I celebrated: _____

WHAT IS THAT?

en wears her pink glasses most of the time. She wears her blue glasses when she's reading
hen she wants to see things close up.

Here is a picture of an object I see every day.
It looks funny because I took the picture close up.

s is a picture of _____.

HELLO DOWN THERE!

One of Karen's favorite things to do is to lie on the ground and look up at the world. See *things from a "worm's-eye view" can be very funny!*

This picture is a worm's-eye view.
I laid down on my back, pointed the camera up, and took a picture.

This is a picture of _____

It was taken on _____

A FAVORITE PHOTO

s is a picture of _____.

was taken on _____.

ONE LAST PHOTO

This is a picture of _____

It was taken on _____